Dietrich Bonhoeffer

Meditation and Prayer

Edited by Peter Frick

LITURGICAL PRESS

Collegeville, Minnesota

www.litpress.org

1	2	3	4	5	6	7	8

Library of Congress Cataloging-in-Publication Data

Bonhoeffer, Dietrich, 1906–1945.
    Dietrich Bonhoeffer : meditation and prayer / edited by
Peter Frick.
        p.   cm.
    Includes bibliographical references.
    ISBN 978-0-8146-3300-7
    1. Spiritual life—Christianity.   2. Prayers.   3. Meditations.
I. Frick, Peter.   II. Title.

BV4501.3.B6627   2010
242—dc22   2009045603

TO WILHELM AND STEFFI

FRIENDS FOREVER
IN TIMES OF PURE JOY
IN MOMENTS OF DEEPEST SORROW

Contents

Acknowledgments

Excerpts from *The Cost of Discipleship* and *Ethics* by Dietrich Bonhoeffer reprinted with the permission of SCM Press. All rights reserved. (World rights in English outside the United States and its territories.)

Excerpts from *Letters and Papers from Prison*. Edited by Eberhard Bethge. Exp. ed. New York: MacMillan Publishing Co., 1971. Used by permission of SCM Press © 1971. (World rights in English outside the United States and its territories.)

Stand-alone quote of 68 words [from the 1996 Fortress Press translation] of ACT AND BEING by DIETRICH BONHOEFFER and TRANSLATED BY BERNARD NOBLE © 1956 by Christian Kaiser Verlag. Translation copyright © 1961 by William Collins Sons & Co. Ltd. and Harper & Brothers Inc. Reprinted by permission of HarperCollins Publishers. (English language rights in North America.)

Preface

Every Christian needs spiritual direction. Dietrich Bonhoeffer knew that he was no exception. One of his Christian mentors was the medieval monk Thomas à Kempis, whose classic work, *The Imitation of Christ*, left a permanent spiritual imprint on Bonhoeffer. In addition to such important matters as following after Jesus Christ and being willing to suffer for the sake of the gospel, à Kempis inspired Bonhoeffer to practice meditation and to engage in disciplined prayer. Not only did Bonhoeffer make it a lifelong habit himself to practice the spiritual disciplines, but he also encouraged other Christians to do the same, especially during his directorship of the underground seminary of the Confessing Church in Finkenwalde from 1935 to 1937. In his book *Life Together*, an account of the spiritual community established in Finkenwalde, Bonhoeffer identifies "three things for which the Christian needs a regular time during the day: *meditation on the Scripture*, *prayer* and *intercession*. All three should find a place in the *daily period of meditation*."[1]

The purpose of this book is thus straightforward: to encourage and help the reader to find his or her way into the daily practice of meditation and prayer. For some readers these practices are not new, and they perhaps need just a gentle reminder. For others, this may be the first attempt into a regular prayer life embedded in the practice of meditation. On the one hand, Bonhoeffer's texts are meant to focus the reader's attention on a specific thought. On the surface, it seems a rather trivial thing to focus our thoughts on one or two particular ideas. Nevertheless, given the general superficiality of our hectic lifestyles, reality for most people is such that it will prove difficult to focus on any thought for an extended time. With patience and over time, the Christian can learn to let his or her mind be focused on a particular thought for the day. These texts can facilitate finding such a focus or can function as a gateway to meditate on passages of Scripture—the ultimate goal of meditation. On the other hand, each session of meditation should naturally lead into a time of prayer. The prayer should be related to the thoughts of the meditation but also include aspects such as intercession for other people, events, and so on. At any rate, the time of meditation should open up the heart and mind to delight in deliberate and regular prayer.

From a practical point of view, it is best to take one of the texts and meditate on it for a few days or an entire week rather than jumping too quickly from one text to the next. The rewards of a lifelong habit of meditation and prayer are subtle but powerful: they provide, in Bonhoeffer's words, "solid ground under our feet" in the midst of life's raging storms.

Peter Frick
Waterloo, Lent 2009

Meditation and Prayer

Behind all needs and lack of direction
stands fundamentally our need for prayer;
for all too long
most of us
were without help and instruction.
Only one thing helps,
to begin anew,
faithfully and patiently
the most basic exercises
in prayer and meditation.[2]

Praying

Prayer is the heart of the Christian life.

Praying is not just asking,
nor is it just giving thanks.

Praying means first of all to become so quiet
that we perceive God's word to us,
and then it means to respond to that word
either in words or in deeds.

Praying means to turn one's life to God
and to his word as revealed to us
through Christ,
to surrender, entrust our lives
completely to God,
to throw ourselves into God's arms,
to grow together with God,
to sense God's life in our own lives.

Praying means wanting
to approach and remain close
to God
because God has come close
to us.[3]

First Thought

The very first moments
of the new day
do not belong
to our plans and sorrows,
nor to the consuming commitments of our work,
but to God's freeing grace,
to God's blessed nearness.[4]

Stillness at Daybreak

Before daybreak,
Jesus prays.
God wants to open up the heart,
before the heart opens up
to the world.
Before the ear
listens to the countless voices of the day,
let it hear
the voice of the Creator and Redeemer
in the early morning.
Stillness at daybreak
God made for himself.
It belongs to him.[5]

Every New Morning

Every new morning
is a new beginning of our life.
Every day
is a completed whole.
This day, today
is the limit of our
sorrows and efforts.
It is long enough
to find God
or to lose him,
to keep faith
or to fall into sin and shame.
Just as the good old sun
rises every morning anew,
so is God's eternal mercy
new every morning.[6]

Being Alone

Every day,
put a few minutes aside to be alone,
and think about the coming day
or the day that has just passed,
about people you have met.
Also think about yourself
and about what you are lacking.
But never brood excessively by yourself;
rather let the One who also knows your secrets
participate in your solitude.
Each of us has things we never utter,
things we conceal
like a beloved treasure within our solitude.
Only God knows them;
hence draw God
into your solitude.[7]

Community and Solitude

Whoever cannot be alone
should beware of community.
Whoever cannot stand being in community
should beware of being alone.

The mark of solitude is silence,
just as speech is the mark of community.
Silence and speech
have the same inner connection and distinction
as being alone and in community.

One does not exist without the other.
Genuine speech comes out of silence,
and genuine silence comes out of speech.[8]

Silence

We are silent
early in the morning
because God should have the first word,
and we are silent before going to bed
because the last word also belongs to God.

We remain silent solely for the sake of the Word.

In the end,
silence means nothing other than waiting
for God's Word
and coming from God's Word
with a blessing.

Real silence,
real stillness,
really holding one's tongue,
comes only as the sober consequence of
spiritual silence.

There is a wonderful
power in being silent
—the power of clarification, purification,
and the focus on what is essential.[9]

Poverty of Prayer

How many
of us
suffer
from this poverty of prayer
and alienation from prayer?
And yet
one thing is certain:
the Christian cause
lives or dies
—with prayer.[10]

Loneliness

I am alone.
There is no one
to whom I can pour out my heart.
I pour it out before myself
and before God.
It is good to pour out one's heart
and not to be consumed
by sorrow and loneliness.
But the greater my loneliness
the greater my desire
to have fellowship with other Christians,
to worship together,
to pray, sing, praise, give thanks and celebrate
together.[11]

The God of Jesus Christ

The God of Jesus Christ
has nothing to do with what God,
as we imagine him,
could do and ought to do.
If we are to learn what God promises,
and what he fulfils,
we must persevere in quiet meditation
on the life, sayings, deeds, sufferings and
    death of Jesus.
It is certain that we may always live close to God
and in the light of his presence,
and that such living is an entirely new life for us;
that nothing is then impossible for us,
because all things are possible with God;
that no earthly power can touch us without his will,
and that danger and distress can only drive us closer
to him.

In Jesus
God has said Yes and Amen
to it all,
and that Yes and Amen
is the firm ground
on which we stand.[12]

Truth

But it can never do any good
to fool oneself into ignoring

the truth,

for in deceiving oneself about the truth
of one's own life
one is certainly deceiving oneself

about God's truth as well.

And it is certainly never pious
to close the eyes that God gave us
to see our neighbor
and his or her need,
simply to avoid seeing whatever
is sad or dreadful.[13]

The Truth

The truth shall make you free.
Perhaps this is the most revolutionary word
in all of the New Testament.

The *truth* shall make you free,
this is extremely unpopular, at all times.

All of us are afraid of the truth.
This anxiety is essentially our anxiety of God.

God's truth is God's love
and God's love frees us from ourselves
for the other.

To be free means nothing else except
being in love.
And being in love means nothing else except
being in God's truth.[14]

Truth and Love

Insight, knowledge, truth
without love is nothing—
it is not even truth,
for truth is God, and God is truth.

So truth without love is a lie; it is nothing.
Truth just for oneself
truth spoken in enmity and hate
is not truth but a lie,
for truth brings us into God's presence,
and God is love.

Truth
is either the clarity of love,
or it is nothing.[15]

Genuine Prayer

We pray to God,
in whom we believe through Christ.
Therefore our prayer
can never be a pleading with God.

Genuine prayer
is not a deed,
an exercise,
a pious attitude.
Rather it is the request of the child
to the heart of the Father.
That is why prayer is never demonstrative,
neither before God,
nor before ourselves,
nor before others.[16]

Mediated Prayer

Anyone who is bound to Jesus
in discipleship
has access to the Father through him.
Thus, every true prayer
is mediated prayer.
There is no such thing as unmediated praying.
Even in prayer
there is no unmediated access to the Father.
Only through Jesus Christ
may we find the Father
in prayer.

He is the only mediator of our prayer.
We pray trusting his word.
So our prayer is always
prayer bound to his word.[17]

Praying for One Another

A Christian community
either lives by the intercessory prayer
of its members for one another,
or the community will be destroyed.

Intercessory prayer
is the purifying bath
into which the individual and the community
must enter every day.

Offering intercessory prayer
means nothing other than Christians bringing one
    another
into the presence of God,
seeing each other under the cross of Jesus
as poor human beings and sinners
in need of grace.[18]

One Step at a Time

Human beings want to understand life
from the beginning to the end.
But God does not allow it.
He wants human beings to go step by step,
guided not by their own ideas of life,
but by God's word,
which comes to them on every step
when they ask.
There is no word of God
for the whole of our life.
God's word is new and free today and tomorrow,
it is only applicable to the very moment
in which we hear it.
God wants us to go step by step
in order to drive us to Himself for help
again and again.[19]

Temptation

Every temptation
is the temptation of Jesus Christ
and every victory
is the victory of Jesus Christ.
Every temptation leads the believer
into deepest loneliness,
into being forsaken
by both human beings and by God.
But in this loneliness one finds Jesus Christ,
who is both
human being and God.
The blood of Christ
and *the example of Christ*
and *the prayer of Christ*
are one's help and strength.[20]

Obedience

Lord,
do not allow us to go around
spouting empty words and pious sayings,
but show us that it is better
to love than to produce words and
better to obey than to argue.
We are always trying to escape from your commands
with words and various pious sayings.
Hold us fast,
take us captive,
compel us
to obey your word,
which is valid for today.
May we do today what we can do today,
and may we do it
in faith.[21]

You Are God's Child

You,
human being,
no matter who you are,

you are God's child,

you are included in God's love,
out of the pure, incomprehensible grace of God;
accept this word, believe in it,
trust in his rule
rather than in yourself or in your own party,
rather than in your own work or your own religion.
God does as he wills.

Turn your misery into God's blessed presence,
and from within your guilt and distress
hear the voice
of the eternal, living God.[22]

Cheap Grace

Cheap grace is the mortal enemy of the church.

Cheap grace
means grace as doctrine,
as principle,
as system.
It means forgiveness of sins
as a general truth;
it means God's love as merely
a Christian idea of God.

Cheap grace
is preaching forgiveness without repentance;
it is baptism without the discipline of community;
it is the Lord's Supper without confession of sin;
it is absolution without personal confession.

Cheap grace
is grace without discipleship,
grace without the cross,
grace without the living, incarnate Jesus Christ.[23]

Good Friday and Easter

Good
Friday
and Easter
free us to think
about other things
far beyond our own personal fate,
about the ultimate meaning
of all life,
suffering,
and events;
and we lay hold
of a great hope.[24]

The Call to Discipleship

Because Jesus is the Christ,
he has authority to call and to demand obedience
to his word.
Jesus calls to discipleship,
not as a teacher and a role model,
but as the Christ,
the Son of God.

Discipleship is commitment to Christ.

Christianity without discipleship
is always Christianity without Jesus Christ.
It is an idea, a myth.[25]

Following Jesus

If people do not follow,
they remain behind,
then they do not learn to believe.
Those called must go out of their situation,
in which they cannot believe,
into a situation in which faith can begin.

The road to faith passes through obedience.

Only the believer obeys—
obedience follows faith,
the way good fruit comes from a good tree.

Only the obedient believe.
A first step of obedience has to be taken,
so that faith does not become pious self-deception,
cheap grace.
The first step is crucial.
Faith is possible only in this new state of existence
created by faith.[26]

Sin

Because the fundamental nature of sin
is to obtain praise for itself
and to judge over good and evil,
sin can never recognize
its own sinfulness.
Sin is thus not a person's judgment
over one's actions,
but sin is *a judgment of God*,
who calls sin that which people call good
—one's own righteousness.[27]

Sinners

Were it really a human possibility
for persons themselves to know that
they are sinners
apart from revelation,
neither "being in Adam" nor "being in Christ"
would be existential designations of their being.
For it would mean
that human beings could place themselves
into truth,
that they could somehow withdraw
to a deeper being of their own,
apart from their being sinners,
their "not being in the truth."[28]

Confession

Is not the reason
for our innumerable relapses and for the feebleness
of our Christian obedience
to be found precisely in the fact
that we are living from self-forgiveness
and not from the real forgiveness of our sins?
Self-forgiveness can never lead to the break with sin.

Only another Christian who is under the cross
can hear my confession.
It is not experience of life
but experience of the cross that makes one suited
to hear confession.

The other believer breaks the circle of self-deception.
Sin must be brought into the light.
Sin that has been spoken and confessed
has lost all of its power.
It has been revealed and judged as sin.[29]

Faith

Faith is
where I give myself completely to God
so that I risk life on account of his word
even and especially
if there seems to be no proof for it.
Only when I forfeit
visible proof
do I have faith in God.
The only certainty
that faith accepts
is the very word of God.[30]

I Believe

I believe
that God will give us all the strength we need
to help us to resist
in all time of distress.
But he never gives it in advance,
lest we should rely on ourselves
and not on him alone.
A faith such as this
should allay all our fears for the future.
I believe
that even our mistakes and shortcomings
are turned to good account,
and that it is no harder for God
to deal with them
than with our supposedly good deeds.
I believe
that God
is no timeless fate,
but that he waits for
and answers sincere prayers
and responsible actions.[31]

Costly Grace

Costly grace
is the hidden treasure in the field,
is the costly pearl,
is Christ's sovereignty,
is the call of Jesus Christ.

Costly grace
is the gospel which must be sought again and again,
the gift which has to be asked for,
the door at which one has to knock.
It is costly, because it calls to discipleship;
it is grace, because it calls us to follow Jesus Christ.
It is costly, because it costs people their lives;
it is grace, because it thereby makes them live.
It is costly, because it condemns sin;
it is grace, because it justifies the sinner.

Above all,
grace is costly,
because it was costly to God,
because it costs God
the life of God's Son.[32]

Believe in God's Grace

Believe in God's grace.
But that means
suddenly having the rug pulled out
from under your feet,
means standing where actually
no person can stand,
means undertaking something infinitely absurd
and infinitely courageous,
means seeing God rather than the world,
means seeing God's abundance
rather than our own misfortune and guilt,
means becoming extremely small
and seeing God become great,
means taking seriously
the incomprehensible contradiction
that God does indeed want
to have something to do with the world—
despite everything,
and means
recognizing that God is greater
than all distress
and greater than our own hearts,
which condemn us.[33]

The Source

The source of a Christian ethic
is not the reality of one's own self,
not the reality of the world,
nor is it the reality of norms and values.
It is the reality of God that is revealed
in Jesus Christ.
With what reality will we reckon in our life?
With the reality of God's revelatory word
or with the so-called realities of life?
With divine grace
or with earthly inadequacies?
With the resurrection
or with death?[34]

The Church

No human being builds the church,
only Christ alone.
Anyone who wants to build the church
is already engaged in a work of destruction.
Such a person will build a temple for idols,
unintentionally and in ignorance.
We shall bear witness—he will build.
We shall preach—he will build.
We shall pray to him—he will build.
Christ gives his church
a great comfort:
You—confess, preach and bear witness about me.
I—will alone build as it pleases me.[35]

Joy

Joy in the sermon,
joy in the sacraments,
joy in the brother and sister
—this is the joy of the believing community
in her invisible, heavenly Lord.

Joy in the sermon
—how difficult it is for us modern people
to find it.
It is because we listen
to the preacher
and not to Christ.

We deprive ourselves of joy
because we confuse heavenly with earthly joy.
Christ offers us heavenly joy
through his weak church.
Let us receive it from him alone
and not from the preacher.
He wants to visit us in the sermon
and be himself our heavenly joy.[36]

Freedom

Freedom
is not a quality that can be uncovered;
it is not a possession,
something to hand, an object;
nor is it a form of something to hand,
instead it is a relation
and nothing else.

To be more precise,
freedom is a relation
between two persons.
Being free
means "being-free-for-the-other,"
because I am bound to the other.
Only by being in relation with the other
am I free.[37]

Spiritual Love

Spiritual love
loves the other
for the sake of Christ.

Spiritual love
comes from Jesus Christ;
it serves him alone.
Christ stands between me and others.
I do not know in advance
what love of others means on the basis
of the general idea of love
that grows out of
my emotional desires.
Jesus Christ will tell me
what love for my brothers and sisters really looks like.
Therefore, spiritual love is bound
to the word of Jesus Christ alone.[38]

Love of Others

I must release others
from all my attempts
to control, coerce, and dominate them
with my love.
In their freedom from me,
other persons want to be loved
for who they are,
as those for whom Christ became a human being,
died, and rose again,
as those for whom Christ won the forgiveness of sins
and prepared eternal life.

This is the meaning of the claim
that we can encounter others only through
the mediation of Christ.[39]

Love as the deed of simple obedience
is death to the old self
and the self's discovery to exist
now
in the righteousness of Christ
and in one's brothers and sisters.[40]

Simplicity of Trust

Nothing is more ruinous for life together
than to mistrust the spontaneity of others
and suspect their motives.
To psychologize and analyze people,
as has become fashionable these days,
is to destroy all trust,
to expose everything decent to public defamation.
It's the revolt of all that is vulgar
against what's free and genuine.
People don't exist to look into the abyss
of each other's hearts—
nor can they—
but to encounter and accept each other
just as they are—
simply, naturally, in courageous trust.[41]

Torment

Lord God,

look down upon your world.
It is a terrible torment.
Hunger and thirst,
no home, no work,
tears and despair;
God, are these the children of your compassion?

Is this the world you created?
We are soon at our end.
We no longer believe, and we no longer hope.

But now come, O God, and end all this misery,
all this suffering,
and if it is your gracious will
that we fall even deeper
into the water,
do not conceal your promise from us
that you will create a new heaven and a new earth,
that you have invited the poor and the miserable,
the troubled and the suffering
into your kingdom.
Today we would still speak about this promise.
God, make us joyous again.
Amen.[42]

Loss of All Strength

The Christian knows
that his strength will desert him
each time
in the hour of temptation.
Therefore, temptation
is the dark hour
that may prove *irrevocable*.
For this reason, a Christian does not seek
the perseverance of strength,
but prays: *do not lead us into temptation*.
In a biblical sense, then,
temptation does *not* mean: *testing of strength*,
but the loss of all strength,
*the defenseless deliverance
into Satan's hands*.[43]

Suffering

It is infinitely easier
to suffer with others than to suffer alone.
It is infinitely easier
to suffer publicly and honorably
than apart and ignominiously.
It is infinitely easier
to suffer through staking one's life
than to suffer spiritually.
Christ suffered
as a free man alone,
apart and in ignominy,
in body and spirit;
and since then
many Christians
have suffered with him.[44]

Apology for the Weak

Christianity

stands or falls

with its revolutionary protest
against violence,
arbitrariness
and pride of power

and with its apologia

for the weak.[45]

Advent

Jesus is at the door, knocking,
in reality, asking you for help
in the figure of the beggar,
in the figure of the degenerate soul
in shabby clothes,
encountering you in every person you meet.
Christ walks the earth
as long as there are people,
as your neighbor,
as the person through whom
God summons you, makes claims on you.
That is the most serious
and most blessed part
of the Advent message.
Christ is the door;
he lives in the form
of those around us.
Will you close the door
or open it
for him?[46]

One Reality

There are not two realities,
but *only one reality*,
and that is God's reality
revealed in Christ
in the reality of the world.
Partaking in Christ,
we stand at the same time in the reality of God
and in the reality of the world.

It is a denial of God's revelation in Jesus Christ
to wish to be "Christian" without being "worldly,"
or to wish to be worldly without seeing and recognizing
the world in Christ.

Hence, there are not two realms,
but only *the one realm of the Christ-reality*,
in which the reality of God
and the reality of the world
are united.[47]

Ultimate Reality

Where God is known by faith
to be the ultimate reality,
the source of my ethical concern will be that God
be known as the good,
even at the risk that I and the world
are revealed not as good,
but as bad through and through.

That God alone is the ultimate reality,
is, however, not an idea meant to sublimate
the actual world,
nor is it the religious perfecting
of a profane worldview.
It is rather a faithful Yes to God's self-witness,
God's revelation.[48]

Worldliness

As reality is *one* in Christ,
so the person who belongs to this Christ-reality
is also a whole.
Worldliness
does not separate one from Christ,
and being Christian
does not separate one from the world.
Belonging completely to Christ,
one stands at the same time
completely in the world.[49]

Ungodliness

Humanity is summoned to share
in God's sufferings
at the hands of a godless world.
Humanity must therefore really live
in the godless world,
without attempting to gloss over
or explain its ungodliness
in some religious way or other.
Humanity must live a "secular" life,
and thereby share in God's suffering.

It is not the religious act that makes
the Christian,
but participation
in the sufferings of God
in the secular life.
That is repentance:
not in the first place thinking
about one's own needs, problems, sins and fears,
but allowing oneself
to be caught up
into the way of Jesus Christ.[50]

Who Stands Fast?

Who stands fast?
Only the people whose final standard is not
their principles, their conscience,
their freedom or their virtue,
but who are ready to sacrifice all this
when they are called
to obedient and responsible action
in faith
and in exclusive allegiance to God—
responsible people,
who try to make their whole life
an answer to the question and call of God.
Where are
these responsible people?[51]

Earthly Future

There are people
who regard it as frivolous,
and some Christians think it is impious
for anyone to hope and prepare
for a better earthly future.
They think that the meaning of present events
is chaos, disorder, and catastrophe;
and in resignation or pious escapism
they surrender all responsibility
for reconstruction and for
future generations.
It may be
that the day of judgment will dawn tomorrow;
in that case,
we shall gladly stop working
for a better future.
But not before.[52]

Blessing the World

The world lives by the blessing of God
and of the righteous and thus has a future.

Blessing means laying one's hand on something and
saying: Despite everything, you belong to God.
This is what we do with the world
that inflicts such suffering on us.
We do not abandon it;
we do not repudiate, despise, or condemn it;
instead we call it back to God,
we give it hope,
we lay our hand on it and say:
may God's blessing come upon you,
may God renew you;
be blessed, world created by God,
you belong to your creator and redeemer.[53]

Being Awake

Being awake means living before God.
Being awake means living with God alone
because he alone is immortal.
This means: arise from the dead—and live!

Do not let anyone put a mask on you;
not the mask of one who knows the art of life
—but is dead behind the mask.
No mask at all!
Not the mask of the eternal seeker,
not the mask of the eternal self-sufficient,
not the mask of the moral nor of the immoral,
not the mask of the pious,
not the mask of the cynic.

But live!
Be alive!
Rise from the dead.
Live before God
as the person
who God created—you.[54]

Waiting

Who, today, is able
to wait, to live into the future
as if the future is the presence,
to live before God
as if he was more certain than my own life?
No one else
except the person who knows
that God, who wants to come, has already come.

God has come.
For this reason alone we can wait,
that he will come, over and over again.
No one has God,
as if there is no more waiting.
And yet, no one can wait for *God*
except in the knowledge
that God
has already waited for us.[55]

God Shows Himself

God does not deceive anyone.
God could bring forth bread,
but then, people would worship him
as their bread provider,
but not as the one he truly is:
as God who is God,
even in hunger,
even in dire needs,
even under the cross,
and even in death.
It is not the love of God
that would thus deceive our knowledge
of who God is.
God shows himself
through himself,
but not through bread.[56]

Be Human Beings

God
wants us to be wholly
what we are.

Be men and women,
both wholly
and in their essence
as created by God.
Be human beings
with your own wills, with your own passions
and your own concerns,
your happiness and your distress,
your seriousness and your frivolity,
your jubilation and your misery.[57]

Eternity

Death
is mighty in the world;
it tears open wounds that never again
completely heal;
it reaps wherever it wants.
It takes the child from its mother's arms,
seizes the young boy at play,
abducts friend from friend,
spouse from spouse,
a brother from his brothers and sisters, mother,
father from children.

Death
is strong over the world,
but love is strong for eternity.
Where there is love, there is eternity,
and there is no more death.
Where human hearts have met
in the most profound, pure, sacred love,
not even a thousand deaths have been able
to separate souls from one another;
there life is lived for eternity.[58]

Epilogue

Now, at the end of the journey through this little book, the reader can look back into the deep treasury of spiritual wisdom as unearthed by Dietrich Bonhoeffer. These texts have achieved their purpose if they have opened up our hearts to engage in regular meditation and mindful prayer, as these are the hallmarks of the normal spiritual life of every Christian. Bonhoeffer understood this more clearly and lived it more profoundly than most other Christians of his time—pastors and theologians included. Two of his books, now considered spiritual classics, are *Discipleship* and *Life Together*. In the first work, he explores what it means for the individual believer to follow Jesus Christ, to take up his cross, and not to cheapen divine grace; in the second work he discusses the characteristics of genuine Christian community such as silence and speech, service, true love, confession, and the Lord's Supper.

Bonhoeffer's interest in the spiritual disciplines may mislead us to think that he was foremost a spiritual mentor. This is not the case. To be sure, there was a phase in his life in the mid-1930s, when he worked with the seminarians in the underground seminary, during which he emphasized spiritual formation. Yet, to read Bonhoeffer as if he were primarily concerned with spiritual tutoring would be a serious misrepresentation of his thought and life as a whole. Bonhoeffer's life and legacy must be appreciated in its complexity and fullness with an understanding of his various roles, such as spiritual mentor, pastor, academic, theologian, and political conspirator. The latter role often functions as another lens through which all of Bonhoeffer's life is seen and judged. The reason for this one-sided appraisal of his life lies in the fact that he is widely known as a man—indeed as a Christian of caliber—who was willing to participate in tyrannicide. This side of Bonhoeffer, the man of the conspiracy and imprisonment, is known to us through his famous *Letters and Papers from Prison*.

In any case, interpreting Bonhoeffer's legacy at the extremes of either spiritual mentor or political conspirator runs the risk of gravely misconstruing his life. He was both spiritual mentor and conspirator, but he was much more than that, as we noted above. In all fairness to his life in its full breadth and depth, a life always lived in fragments and in unusual times, it is indispensable to get to know the real Bonhoeffer, embedded as he was in countless and ever-changing contexts and situations.

Given the scope and limit of this book, the texts presented here show us Bonhoeffer as the spiritual mentor.

Nonetheless, it is my hope that some readers may be persuaded to become interested in Bonhoeffer in a broader and more comprehensive manner. With this aim in view, the reader will find a good number of primary and secondary sources below. For a comprehensive portrait of Bonhoeffer to emerge, most important is the reading of primary sources, for in these writings we hear his own voice. In addition, there is also a brief listing of representative secondary works. This list is not comprehensive and is meant to be a mere pointer to the vast amount of literature on Bonhoeffer. It is a long and not always easy journey to embark on, quite literally a mountain of reading, but it is certainly worth the persistence. For in the life of Bonhoeffer we meet a Christian whose words exposed many false gods and whose deeds never strayed from the path of Jesus Christ.

Endnotes

[1] Dietrich Bonhoeffer. *Life Together and The Prayerbook of the Bible: An Introduction to the Psalms*. Edited by G. Kelly. Translated by D. Bloesch and J. Burtness (Minneapolis, MN: Fortress Press, 1996), 86; emphasis in original; hereafter *DBWE* 5. Cf. à Kempis: "Set aside an opportune time for deep personal reflection and think often about God's many benefits to you. Give up all light and frivolous matters, and read what inspires you to repentance of soul and not what just entertains the mind. If you abstain from unnecessary conversation and useless visiting, as well as from listening to idle news and gossip, you will find sufficient and suitable times for your meditation" (Thomas à Kempis. *The Imitation of Christ*. Translated by Joseph Tylenda [New York: Random House, Inc., 1998], I 20, 1).

[2] Dietrich Bonhoeffer. *Illegale Theologenausbildung: Finkenwalde 1935–1937*. Edited by Otto Dudzus and Jürgen Henkys with Sabine Bobert-Stützel, Dirk Schulz, and Ilse Tödt (Gütersloh: Chr. Kaiser/Gütersloher Verlagshaus, 1996), 950, my translation; hereafter *DBW* 14.

[3] Dietrich Bonhoeffer. *Barcelona, Berlin, New York: 1928–1931*. Edited by C. Green. Translated by D. W. Stott (Minneapolis, MN: Fortress Press, 2008), 577; hereafter *DBWE* 10.

[4] *DBW* 14, 872; my translation.

[5] *DBW* 14, 872–73; my translation.

[6] *DBW* 14, 871; my translation.

[7] *DBWE* 10, 554.

[8] *DBWE* 5, 83.

9 *DBWE* 5, 85.

10 *DBWE* 10, 577.

11 *DBW* 14, 854–55; my translation.

12 Dietrich Bonhoeffer. *Letters and Papers from Prison.* Edited by Eberhard Bethge (New York: Collier Books, Macmillan Publishing, enlarged edition, 1971), 391. Reprinted with the permission of Scribner, a Division of Simon & Schuster, Inc., from LETTERS AND PAPERS FROM PRISON, REVISED, ENLARGED ED. by Dietrich Bonhoeffer (Translated from the German by R. H. Fuller, Frank Clark, et al.). Copyright © 1953, 1967, 1971 by SCM Press Ltd. All rights reserved. (English language rights in the United States and its territories.)

13 Dietrich Bonhoeffer. *London: 1933–1935.* Edited by Keith Clements. Translated by Isabel Best (Minneapolis, MN: Fortress Press, 2007), 366; hereafter *DBWE* 13.

14 Dietrich Bonhoeffer, *Ökumene, Universität, Pfarramt 1931–1932.* Edited by Eberhard Amelung and Christoph Strohm (Gütersloh: Chr. Kaiser/Gütersloher Verlagshaus, 1994), 454, 456, 458, 461, my translation; hereafter *DBW* 11.

15 *DBWE* 13, 380.

16 Dietrich Bonhoeffer. *Discipleship.* Edited by G. Kelly and J. Godsey. Translated by B. Green and R. Krauss (Minneapolis, MN: Fortress Press, 2001), 153; hereafter *DBWE* 4. Reprinted with the permission of Scribner, a Division of Simon & Schuster, Inc., from *The Cost of Discipleship* by Dietrich Bonhoeffer. Copyright © 1959 by SCM Press Ltd. All rights reserved. (English language rights in the United States and its territories.)

17 *DBWE* 4, 153.

18 *DBWE* 5, 90.

19 *DBWE* 13, 399; translation slightly altered.

[20] Dietrich Bonhoeffer. *Illegale Theologenausbildung: Sammelvikariate 1937–1940*. Edited by Dirk Schulz (Gütersloh: Chr. Kaiser/Gütersloher Verlagshaus, 1998), 404; my translation. Hereafter *DBW* 15.

[21] *DBWE* 13, 411.

[22] *DBWE* 13, 359.

[23] *DBWE* 4, 43–44.

[24] *Letters and Papers from Prison*, 25.

[25] *DBWE* 4, 57–58.

[26] *DBWE* 4, 63–64.

[27] *DBW* 15, 331; my translation.

[28] Dietrich Bonhoeffer. *Act and Being: Transcendental Philosophy and Ontology in Systematic Theology.* Edited by Wayne W. Floyd. Translated by H. Martin Rumscheidt (Minneapolis, MN: Fortress Press, 1996), 136.

[29] *DBWE* 5, 112, 113, 115.

[30] Dietrich Bonhoeffer. *Berlin: 1932–1933.* Edited by Carsten Nicolaisen and Ernst-Albert Scharffenorth (Gütersloh: Chr. Kaiser/ Gütersloher Verlagshaus, 1997), 346; my translation. Hereafter *DBW* 12.

[31] *Letters and Papers from Prison*, 11.

[32] *DBWE* 4, 44–45.

[33] *DBWE* 10, 525–26.

[34] Dietrich Bonhoeffer. *Ethics*. Edited by C. Green. Translated by R. Krauss, C. West, and D. W. Stott (Minneapolis, MN: Fortress Press, 2005), 49; hereafter *DBWE* 6. Reprinted with the permission of Scribner, a Division of Simon & Schuster, Inc., from *Ethics* by Dietrich Bonhoeffer. Copyright © 1955 by SCM Press Ltd. by Macmillan Publishing Company. All rights reserved. (English language rights in the United States and its territories.)

[35] *DBW* 12, 469; my translation.

[36] *DBW* 12, 457; my translation.

[37] Dietrich Bonhoeffer. *Creation and Fall: A Theological Exposition of Genesis 1–3*. Edited by John de Gruchy. Translated by D. Bax (Minneapolis, MN: Fortress Press, 1997), 63.

[38] *DBWE* 5, 43.

[39] *DBWE* 5, 44.

[40] *DBWE* 4, 152.

[41] Dietrich Bonhoeffer. *Fiction from Tegel Prison*. Edited by C. Green. Translated by Nancy Lukens (Minneapolis, MN: Fortress Press, 2000), 65–66.

[42] *DBWE* 10, 536; translation slightly altered.

[43] *DBW* 15, 373; my translation.

[44] *Letters and Papers from Prison*, 14.

[45] *DBWE* 13, 402.

[46] *DBWE* 10, 545.

[47] *DBWE* 6, 58.

[48] *DBWE* 6, 48.

[49] *DBWE* 6, 62.

[50] *Letters and Papers from Prison*, 361.

[51] *Letters and Papers from Prison*, 5; translation slightly altered.

[52] *Letters and Papers from Prison*, 15–16.

[53] Dietrich Bonhoeffer. *Conspiracy and Imprisonment: 1940–1945*. Edited by Mark S. Brocker. Translated by Lisa E. Dahill and D. W. Stott (Minneapolis, MN: Fortress Press, 2006), 632.

[54] *DBW* 11, 465; my translation.

[55] *DBW* 11, 393; my translation.

[56] *DBW* 11, 397; my translation.

[57] *DBWE* 10, 530.

[58] *DBWE* 10, 538.

Recommended Reading

The most important edition of primary texts is the seventeen-volume German edition, *Dietrich Bonhoeffer Werke*, abbreviated as *DBW* (1986–1998). This series is currently being translated into and edited as the critical English edition under the auspices of the International Bonhoeffer Society (*Dietrich Bonhoeffer Works English*, abbreviated as *DBWE*) in cooperation with Fortress Press, Minneapolis. Any person who is interested in Bonhoeffer on a deeper level must turn to these volumes. The following volumes are already published; the remaining ones are in preparation.

Primary Texts

Vol. 1 *Sanctorum Communio: A Theological Study of the Sociology of the Church.* Edited by C. Green. Translated by R. Krauss and N. Lukens. Minneapolis, MN: Fortress Press, 1998.

Vol. 2 *Act and Being: Transcendental Philosophy and Ontology in Systematic Theology.* Edited by Wayne W. Floyd. Translated by H. Martin Rumscheidt. Minneapolis, MN: Fortress Press, 1996.

Vol. 3 *Creation and Fall: A Theological Exposition of Genesis 1–3.* Edited by John de Gruchy. Translated by D. Bax. Minneapolis, MN: Fortress Press, 1997.

Vol. 4 *Discipleship.* Edited by G. Kelly and J. Godsey. Translated by B. Green and R. Krauss. Minneapolis, MN: Fortress Press, 2000.

Vol. 5 *Life Together and The Prayerbook of the Bible: An Introduction to the Psalms.* Edited by G. Kelly. Translated by D. Bloesch and J. Burtness. Minneapolis, MN: Fortress Press, 1996.

Vol. 6 *Ethics.* Edited by C. Green. Translated by R. Krauss, C. West, and D. W. Stott. Minneapolis, MN: Fortress Press, 2005.

Vol. 7 *Fiction from Tegel Prison.* Edited by C. Green. Translated by Nancy Lukens. Minneapolis, MN: Fortress Press, 2000.

Vol. 9 *The Young Bonhoeffer: 1918–1927.* Edited by Paul D. Matheny, C. Green, and M. D. Johnson. Translated by Mary Nebelsick and D. W. Stott. Minneapolis, MN: Fortress Press, 2003.

Vol. 10 *Barcelona, Berlin, New York: 1928–1931.* Edited by C. Green. Translated by D. W. Stott. Minneapolis, MN: Fortress Press, 2008.

Vol. 13 *London: 1933–1935.* Edited by Keith Clements. Translated by Isabel Best. Minneapolis, MN: Fortress Press, 2007.

Vol. 16 *Conspiracy and Imprisonment: 1940–1945.* Edited by Mark S. Brocker. Translated by Lisa E. Dahill and D. W. Stott. Minneapolis, MN: Fortress Press, 2006.

Letters and Papers from Prison. Edited by Eberhard Bethge. Exp. ed. New York: MacMillan Publishing Co., 1971.

Love Letters from Cell 92: The Correspondence between Dietrich Bonhoeffer and Maria von Wedemeyer, 1943–1945. Translated by John Brownjohn. Nashville, TN: Abingdon, 1995.

Secondary Texts

The following is a list of some secondary sources on Bonhoeffer in English that will guide the reader along the path of discovery in a reliable manner. This bibliography is by no means exhaustive; there are many other excellent works on Bonhoeffer.

Bethge, Eberhard. *Dietrich Bonhoeffer: Theologian, Christian, Man for His Times: A Biography*. Edited by Victoria Barnett. Translated by Eric Mosbacher. Minnesota, MN: Fortress Press, 2000.

Dahill, Lisa. *Reading from the Underside of Selfhood: Bonhoeffer and Spiritual Formation*. Eugene, OR: Pickwick, 2009.

De Gruchy, John W., ed. *The Cambridge Companion to Dietrich Bonhoeffer*. Cambridge: Cambridge University Press, 1999.

———, ed. *Dietrich Bonhoeffer: Witness to Jesus Christ*. London: Collins, 1988.

Dramm, Sabine. *Dietrich Bonhoeffer: An Introduction to his Thought*. Peabody, MA: Hendrickson, 2007.

Feil, Ernst. *The Theology of Dietrich Bonhoeffer*. Translated by H. M. Rumscheidt. Philadelphia, PA: Fortress Press, 1985.

Floyd, Wayne Whitson, Jr. *Theology and the Dialectics of Otherness: On Reading Bonhoeffer and Adorno*. Lanham, MD: University Press of America, 1988.

Frick, Peter, ed. *Bonhoeffer's Intellectual Formation: Theology and Philosophy in His Thought*. Tübingen: Mohr Siebeck, 2008.

Green, Clifford. *Bonhoeffer: A Theology of Sociality*. Rev. ed. Grand Rapids, MI: William B. Eerdmans, 1999.

Haynes, Stephen. *The Bonhoeffer Phenomenon: Portraits of a Protestant Saint*. Minneapolis, MN: Fortress Press, 2004.

Kelly, Geffrey B., and F. Burton Nelson, eds. *The Cost of Moral Leadership: The Spirituality of Dietrich Bonhoeffer.* Grand Rapids, MI: William B. Eerdmans, 2003.

Lange, Frederik de. *Waiting for the Word: Dietrich Bonhoeffer on Speaking about God.* Grand Rapids, MI: William B. Eerdmans, 2000.

Marsh, Charles. *Reclaiming Dietrich Bonhoeffer: The Promise of His Theology.* New York: Oxford, 1994.

Matthews, John. *Anxious Souls Will Ask: The Christ-centered Spirituality of Dietrich Bonhoeffer.* Grand Rapids, MI: William B. Eerdmans, 2005.

Plant, Stephen. *Bonhoeffer*. New York: Continuum, 2004.

Rasmussen, Larry L. *Dietrich Bonhoeffer: Reality and Resistance.* Nashville/New York: Westminster, 1972.

Rasmussen, Larry L., with Renate Bethge. *Dietrich Bonhoeffer: His Significance for North Americans*. Minneapolis, MN: Fortress Press, 1990.

Wind, Renate. *Dietrich Bonhoeffer: A Spoke in the Wheel*. Grand Rapids, MI: William B. Eerdmans, 1992.

Wüstenberg, Ralf K. *A Theology of Life: Dietrich Bonhoeffer's Religionless Christianity*. Translated by Doug Stott. Grand Rapids, MI/Cambridge: William B. Eerdmans, 1998.

Young, Josiah. *No Difference in the Fare: Dietrich Bonhoeffer and the Problem of Racism*. Grand Rapids, MI: William B. Eerdmans, 1998.